Sundaes & SPLITS

Sundaes & SPLITS

DELICIOUS RECIPES FOR ICE CREAM TREATS

HANNAH MILES   photography by Kate Whitaker

RYLAND
PETERS
& SMALL

LONDON NEW YORK

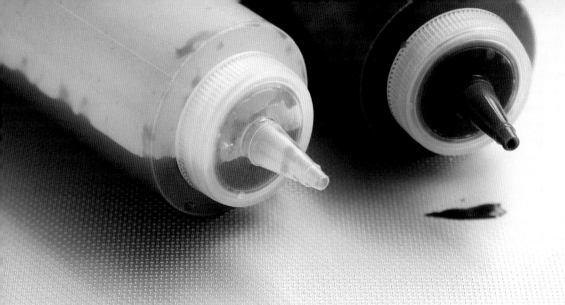

For my brother Gareth, sweet collector extraordinaire.

Design, photographic art direction and prop styling Steve Painter
Senior Commissioning Editor Julia Charles
Head of Production Patricia Harrington
Art Director Leslie Harrington
Publishing Director Alison Starling

Food Stylist Sunil Vijayaker
Indexer Hilary Bird

First published in the United Kingdom in 2010 by Ryland Peters & Small
20–21 Jockey's Fields
London WC1R 4BW
www.rylandpeters.com

10 9 8 7 6 5 4 3 2

Text © Hannah Miles 2010
Design and photographs
© Ryland Peters & Small 2010

Printed in China

ISBN: 978 1 84597 970 6

A CIP record for this book is available from the British Library.

Notes
• All spoon measurements are level unless otherwise specified.
• All eggs are medium.

Author's Acknowledgements
With heartfelt thanks and gratitude to Julia Charles, who loves ice cream as much as I do, believed in the idea for this book and showed unending patience during editing. Grateful thanks also go to all at Ryland Peters & Small, and in particular to Steve Painter for the inspirational styling and design, Kate Whitaker for the stunning photographs and Sunil and Aya for creating perfect sundaes on shoot – you brought my book to life – thank you all x. Love and thanks also go to Heather and Elly of HHB Agency whose friendship over the last two years has meant so much; my good friend Jess for all 'pre-production' test shots and design ideas; my Mum and Dad and all my family and friends for your love and support; my husband Sacha, who tolerates far more mess in the kitchen than any man should have to and yet still loves me. Huge thanks also to my wonderful ice cream tasters: David, Lucy, Kathie, Peter, Susan, Jana, Pam, Steve, Miles, Joshua and Rosie; my hens for the hundreds of eggs used in the recipes and the readers of my blog (hannahscountrykitchen.blogspot.com) who have been with me every step of the way!

Contents

Indulgent treats for everyone

No matter how old you are, there are few things more tempting and deliciously naughty than an ice cream sundae – I have yet to meet anyone who doesn't delight in an elegant glass dish filled with ice creams, sauces, syrups, fruit and whipped cream. This book has ideas for sundaes to suit all tastes; whether you prefer a light and fruity dessert with tangy sorbet or an indulgent treat laden with sticky sauce and creamy ice cream, there is a perfect sundae here for everyone to enjoy.

Making your own delicious ice creams and sorbets at home is an easy process; it just takes a little time and patience. There are many good-quality ice cream machines available – some contain a freezer unit which enables you to churn ice cream almost instantly and others contain a freezer bowl that requires you to freeze it for about 6–8 hours. If you do not have an ice cream machine, you can still make ice cream and sorbets at home. Simply place your prepared mixture in a lidded freezerproof box and pop it in the freezer. Remove from the freezer every hour or so, transfer to a large bowl and whisk with an electric hand mixer or whisk to incorporate air and break up any large ice crystals. This will help give a light and creamy texture. Repeat this every hour until the ice cream is frozen.

The beauty of ice cream is that it can be prepared in advance and will keep well in the freezer for about two months. While many of the recipes in this book are made with home-made ice creams and sorbets, you can substitute good-quality shop-bought versions if you are short of time – the results will be almost as impressive as it's the inspired flavour and texture combinations that make these sundaes so irresistible. So why not treat your friends and family to one of these lip-smacking, ice-cold combinations today?

Vanilla Ice Cream

The key to a good ice cream is a rich creamy base. This basic recipe is used throughout the book and, with the addition of whatever ingredients you choose to add, you can create a wonderful array of interesting flavours.

1 vanilla pod
200 ml whole milk
400 ml double cream
100 g caster sugar
5 egg yolks

Makes 650 ml

Split the vanilla pod lengthways using a sharp knife and then run the back of the knife along the length of each half of the pod to remove the black seeds. Place the seeds, pod halves, milk and cream in a heavy-based saucepan and bring to the boil. Immediately remove from the heat and leave to infuse for 15–20 minutes. Meanwhile whisk together the sugar and egg yolks until light and creamy and doubled in size. Remove the vanilla pod from the milk and cream mixture, bring it to the boil again and then, while still whisking, slowly pour it into the sugar and egg mixture. Return this custard mixture to the pan and over a gentle heat, whisk for a few minutes until the mixture begins to thicken. Set aside until the mixture has cooled completely, then transfer to the fridge to chill. When chilled, add any flavourings to the base and churn in an ice cream machine until frozen (according to the manufacturer's instructions), or you can freeze using the by-hand method given on page 6.

Strawberry

Prepare the Vanilla Ice Cream base according to the method given left. Let cool then blitz in a blender until smooth with 400 g hulled fresh strawberries and a few drops of pink food colouring (optional). Churn or freeze as in main recipe.

Chocolate

Prepare the Vanilla Ice Cream base according to the method given left. Let cool then stir in 200 g melted dark chocolate. Churn or freeze as in main recipe.

Simple Sauces

One of the main elements to a sundae or split is a delicious sauce. A bowl of simple vanilla ice cream can be transformed into a luxurious dessert with a drizzle of home-made chocolate, toffee or summer berry sauce. These sauces can all be stored in the refrigerator for a few days. For most of the sundae recipes in this book, the sauces should be cooled completely before using, however they can be served warm over the ice cream of your choice for an instant hot sundae if you wish.

Chocolate

2 tablespoons golden syrup
100 ml double cream
100 g dark chocolate
30 g unsalted butter

Makes about 300 ml

Place all the ingredients together in a heavy-based saucepan and whisk over a gentle heat until the chocolate has melted and the sauce is smooth and glossy.

Leave the sauce to cool completely before using.

Toffee

80 g light brown sugar
40 g dark brown sugar
200 ml double cream
60 g unsalted butter
1 tablespoon golden syrup

Makes about 450 ml

Place all the ingredients together in a heavy-based saucepan and whisk over gentle heat until the butter has melted, the sugar dissolved and the sauce is smooth and thick.

Leave the sauce to cool completely before using.

Summer berry

1 vanilla pod or 1 teaspoon vanilla extract
250 g fresh strawberries, hulled
150 g fresh raspberries
100 g caster sugar

Makes about 500 ml

Cut the vanilla pod in half lengthways using a sharp knife. Place all the ingredients in a saucepan with 200 ml water and simmer for 8–10 minutes, until the strawberries are very soft and the sugar has dissolved. Strain the sauce through a fine mesh sieve, pressing the fruit down with the back of a spoon to release all the juices. Discard the fruit and leave the sauce to cool completely before using.

FRUITY

Peach melba sundae

This classic combination of sharp raspberries and juicy ripe peaches with a hint of vanilla hardly needs an introduction. It is said to have been invented by the great chef Auguste Escoffier for the soprano Dame Nellie Melba, who loved ice cream but was concerned that the coldness might damage her voice. Escoffier solved this problem by serving the ice cream with fruit to diminish the coldness and in doing so created one of the all time favourite ice cream desserts.

4 ripe peaches, stoned and sliced
120 ml Amaretto di Saronno liqueur
300 ml Summer Berry Sauce (see page 9)
1 quantity Vanilla Ice Cream (see page 8)
200 g fresh raspberries
200 ml double cream, whipped
60 g Amaretti biscuits, crushed

RASPBERRY SORBET:
350 g fresh raspberries
100 g caster sugar
freshly squeezed juice of 1 lemon

an ice cream machine (optional)
4 glass sundae dishes

Serves 4

To make the Raspberry Sorbet, place the raspberries, sugar and lemon juice in a saucepan and add 250 ml water. Simmer for 10–15 minutes over gentle heat until the sugar has dissolved and the raspberries are soft. Strain the mixture through a fine mesh sieve to remove the raspberry seeds and leave to cool completely. Churn in an ice cream machine according to the manufacturer's instructions, or freeze using the by-hand method given on page 6. Freeze until needed.

Place the peach slices in a bowl, pour over the Amaretto and leave the fruit to marinate for about 1 hour.

To assemble, reserve 4 marinated peach slices for decoration and divide the remaining slices between the sundae dishes. Drizzle with a little Summer Berry Sauce. Add a scoop of Vanilla Ice Cream and Raspberry Sorbet to each dish and add a quarter of the raspberries. Drizzle over some more sauce and top with a second scoop of ice cream. Spoon whipped cream onto each sundae and add the reserved peach slices and the rest of the raspberries. Scatter the crushed Amaretti biscuits over the top. Serve immediately.

Pear and ginger sundae

Pear and ginger is a flavour match made in heaven. Here, juicy pears are poached in ginger wine with bay leaves and honey and served with a refreshing pear sorbet and rich stem ginger ice cream.

POACHED PEARS:

4 small ripe pears, peeled, stalks intact

2 tablespoons honey, plus extra to drizzle

a 1-cm piece of fresh ginger, peeled

1 bay leaf

1 cinnamon stick

freshly squeezed juice of ½ a lemon

100 ml ginger wine

PEAR SORBET AND TUILES:

5 small ripe pears

150 g caster sugar

50 ml ginger wine

freshly squeezed juice of 1½ lemons

STEM GINGER ICE CREAM:

80 g stem ginger preserved in syrup, plus 2 tablespoons of the ginger syrup

1 quantity Vanilla Ice Cream base (see page 8), chilled

an ice cream machine (optional)
a baking tray lined with baking paper
4 glass sundae dishes

Serves 4

To make the poached pears, cut the bottom off each peeled pear with a sharp knife so that they sit upright. Using an apple corer, remove the core from the base end, leaving the stalks intact. Place the pears in a saucepan and cover with water. Add the honey, ginger, bay leaf, cinnamon stick, lemon juice and ginger wine. Simmer, uncovered, for 20–30 minutes until the pears are soft. Leave to cool completely in the poaching liquid then chill in the refrigerator until needed.

To make the Pear Sorbet, peel and core 4 of the pears and place them in a saucepan with 300 ml water, the caster sugar, ginger wine and two thirds of the lemon juice. Simmer for 20–25 minutes, until the pears are very soft. Allow to cool then blend with a hand blender to a smooth purée. Churn in an ice cream machine according to the manufacturer's instructions, or freeze using the by-hand method given on page 6. Freeze until needed.

To make the pear tuiles, preheat the oven to 120°C (250°F) Gas ½. Thinly slice the remaining pear, using a mandolin if you have one. Put the pear slices on the prepared baking tray. Brush with the remaining lemon juice and bake in the preheated oven for 2–3 hours, turning half way through cooking, until they are crisp and slightly translucent.

To make the Stem Ginger Ice Cream, finely chop the stem ginger, reserve a little to decorate and stir the remainder into the Vanilla Ice Cream base along with the ginger syrup. Churn in an ice cream machine according to the manufacturer's instructions, or freeze using the by-hand method given on page 6. Freeze until needed.

To assemble, put scoops of Ginger Ice Cream and Pear Sorbet in the sundae dishes. Top each sundae with a poached pear and decorate with the Pear Tuiles. Drizzle the pears with a little honey and sprinkle with the reserved stem ginger to decorate. Serve immediately.

Hawaiian sundae

My idea of a perfect summer holiday is lying by an azure-blue swimming pool, sipping a Piña Colada. This fun sundae takes all the elements of the popular tropical cocktail – rum, coconut and fresh pineapple – and encapsulates them in a refreshing ice cream sundae. Top the sundaes with kitsch cocktail umbrellas or similar and your friends won't be able to resist!

300 g fresh pineapple
200 ml coconut rum, such as Malibu
200 ml double cream, whipped
toasted coconut flakes, to decorate

COCONUT ICE CREAM:
3 egg yolks
100 g caster sugar
400 ml coconut milk
200 ml double cream

PINEAPPLE SORBET:
400 g fresh pineapple
100 ml coconut rum, such as Malibu
200 g caster sugar

an ice cream machine (optional)
4 glass sundae dishes

Serves 4

To make the Coconut Ice Cream, whisk together the egg yolks with the caster sugar until they are light and creamy and have doubled in size. Place the coconut milk and the double cream in a saucepan and bring to the boil. Slowly pour the boiled milk over the whisked egg yolks, continuing to whisk all the time. Allow to cool completely. Churn in an ice cream machine according to the manufacturer's instructions, or freeze using the by-hand method given on page 6. Freeze until needed.

To prepare the Pineapple Sorbet, place the pineapple in a blender with 100 ml water, the coconut rum and caster sugar and blitz to a pulp. Leave to stand for 30 minutes so that the sugar dissolves. Churn in an ice cream machine according to the manufacturer's instructions, or freeze using the by-hand method given on page 6. Freeze until needed.

Chop the remaining pineapple into small pieces and soak in the rum for about 30 minutes.

To assemble, divide half of the marinated pineapple between the sundae dishes. Top with a scoop each of Coconut Ice Cream and Pineapple Sorbet. Cover with the remaining marinated pineapple and then add more ice cream and sorbet. Top each sundae with a quarter of the whipped cream. Decorate with toasted coconut flakes and cocktail umbrellas. Serve immediately.

Melon sundae

Chilled melon is so refreshing on a hot day. Frozen into delicious sorbets, this sundae looks as pretty as a picture with its vibrant 'traffic light' colours. If you are short of time, you can make just one of the melon sorbets and serve it with fresh melons balls instead of making all three.

700 g caster sugar
1 cantaloupe melon (about 550 g flesh)
½ ripe watermelon (about 450 g flesh)
1 galia melon (about 550 g flesh)
1 tablespoon rose syrup
freshly squeezed juice of 2 lemons
freshly squeezed juice of 2 limes

an ice cream machine (optional)
a melon baller
4 glass sundae dishes

Serves 4

To make the Melon Sorbets, place the caster sugar in a large saucepan with 600 ml water and simmer over a gentle heat for 10–15 minutes, until the sugar has dissolved and you have a thin syrup. Allow to cool completely.

Reserve a quarter of each quantity of melon to use for melon balls and roughly chop the remaining flesh.

Divide the cooled sugar syrup between 3 separate bowls. Add the chopped cantaloupe melon to the first, along with the rose syrup and half of the lemon juice. Blend to a smooth purée using a hand-held blender. Add the chopped watermelon to the second bowl along with the lime juice and blend to a smooth purée as before. Finally, add the chopped galia melon to the third bowl, along with the remaining lemon juice and blend to a smooth purée as before.

Churn each melon purée separately in an ice cream machine according to the manufacturer's instructions, or freeze using the by-hand method given on page 6. Freeze until needed.

Scoop the reserved melon flesh into small balls using a melon baller. Place scoops of the 3 sorbets in the sundae dishes in layers with the melon balls inbetween. Serve immediately.

Autumn harvest sundae

With the arrival of autumn comes an abundance of my favourite fruits – sweet apples and ripe juicy blackberries. Take a basket and pick fresh berries from the hedgerows if you can. I've paired these delicious autumnal flavours with warming cinnamon ice cream here to make a sophisticated sundae that perfectly celebrates nature's bounty,

CINNAMON ICE CREAM:

1 quantity Vanilla Ice Cream base with the vanilla omitted (see page 8)

2 cinnamon sticks

2 teaspoons ground cinnamon

BLACKBERRY SORBET:

300 g fresh blackberries plus about 200 g more to serve

115 g caster sugar

1 teaspoon vanilla extract

APPLE PURÉE:

5 green eating apples, peeled, cored and chopped

60 g light brown sugar

freshly squeezed juice of ½ a lemon

an ice cream machine (optional)
4 glass sundae dishes

Serves 4

To make the Cinnamon Ice Cream, omit the vanilla pod from the Vanilla Ice Cream base recipe and replace with the cinnamon sticks and ground cinnamon. Heat the milk and cream with the ground cinnamon and sticks and bring to the boil. Leave to infuse for 15–20 minutes and then remove the cinnamon sticks. Continue following the recipe for Vanilla Ice Cream.

To make the Blackberry Sorbet, put the blackberries in a saucepan with the caster sugar, vanilla and 250 ml water and simmer over gentle heat for about 10 minutes, until the blackberries are very soft. Strain through a fine mesh sieve, pressing down with the back of a spoon to ensure all the juices are released. Allow to cool completely then churn in an ice cream machine according to the manufacturer's instructions, or freeze using the by-hand method given on page 6. Freeze until needed.

To make the Apple Purée, put the apples in a saucepan with the light brown sugar, lemon juice and 300 ml water. Simmer for about 15–20 minutes, until the apple is soft and puréed. Leave to cool completely.

To assemble, divide the cooled apple purée between the sundae dishes. Add a generous scoop of Cinnamon Ice Cream and divide the blackberries between each dish. Top with a scoop of Blackberry Sorbet and serve immediately.

Plum crumble sundae

This comforting sundae, with cinnamon-infused plum compote, ruby-red plum sorbet, cinnamon ice cream and buttery crumble topping, is a must for fruit crumble lovers everywhere! You could also try it with Vanilla Ice Cream (see page 8), Rhubarb Sorbet and poached rhubarb (see page 22).

1 quantity Cinnamon Ice Cream
(page 18)

PLUM SORBET AND COMPOTE:
650 g ripe red plums, quartered
and stoned
100 g caster sugar
1 cinnamon stick

CRUMBLE TOPPING:
140 g plain flour
1 teaspoon ground cinnamon
90 g unsalted butter
60 g light brown sugar

an ice cream machine (optional)
a 20 x 25 cm baking tin, greased

Serves 4

To make the Plum Sorbet, put the plum quarters in a saucepan with the caster sugar, cinnamon stick and 150 ml water. Simmer for 20–25 minutes until the plums are soft. Remove the cinnamon stick and allow the plums to cool completely. Remove a quarter of the plums to use as plum compote in the sundae and purée the remaining plums with a hand blender. Churn the plum purée in an ice cream machine according to the manufacturer's instructions, or freeze using the by-hand method given on page 6. Freeze until needed.

To make the Crumble Topping, preheat the oven to 180°C (350°F) Gas 4. Put the flour and ground cinnamon in a mixing bowl and rub in the butter with your fingertips until the mixture resembles fine breadcrumbs. Stir in the sugar and spoon the mixture into the prepared baking tin. Bake in the preheated oven for 15–20 minutes until golden brown. Leave to cool completely.

Divide the plum compote between the sundae dishes. Top with a few scoops each of Cinnamon Ice Cream and Plum Sorbet. Sprinkle a generous amount of crumble over each sundae and serve immediately.

Rhubarb and custard sundae

Tangy sharp rhubarb and rich creamy custard is a classic taste combination. Topped with curly rhubarb tuiles, this candy-coloured sundae makes an unusual and fun dessert.

RHUBARB SORBET AND TUILES:
800 g pink rhubarb
freshly squeezed juice of 2 lemons
200 g plus 1 tablespoon caster sugar
a few drops of pink food colouring (optional)
1 tablespoon rose syrup

CUSTARD ICE CREAM:
500 g ready-made custard
150 ml double cream

an ice cream machine (optional)
a baking tray, lined with baking paper
4 glass sundae dishes

Serves 4

Using a vegetable peeler, peel all the sticks of rhubarb. Thinly slice 2 of the sticks into long strips using the peeler (for the tuiles). Place these in a saucepan of water with half the lemon juice and the 1 tablespoon caster sugar. Add a few drops of food colouring, if using. Simmer for 2–3 minutes and then transfer to the prepared baking tray and leave to dry overnight. In the morning the rhubarb will be dried but still flexible. Twist each strip of rhubarb into a spiral around the handle of a wooden spoon, gently remove and leave to dry in spirals for a further few hours.

To make the Rhubarb Sorbet, chop the remaining rhubarb into 3-cm pieces. Place in a saucepan with 500 ml water, the rose syrup and the remaining lemon juice. Simmer for 5–7 minutes over a gentle heat until the rhubarb is soft. Remove one third of the rhubarb and set aside to cool. Simmer the remaining rhubarb for a further 5 minutes until it is really soft. Blitz with a hand blender and churn in an ice cream machine according to the manufacturer's instructions, or freeze using the by-hand method given on page 6. Freeze until needed.

To make the Custard Ice Cream, lightly whisk together the custard and double cream and transfer to an ice cream machine. Churn according to the manufacturer's instructions, or freeze using the by-hand method given on page 6. Freeze until needed.

Spoon a little Custard Ice Cream into each sundae dish. Divide the poached rhubarb between them, top with some more ice cream and add a ball of Rhubarb Sorbet. Decorate with the rhubarb tuiles and serve immediately.

INDULGENT

Cookies and cream sundae

There are few more popular ice creams than cookies and cream – it sits at number five in the world ranking of favourite flavours and was the fastest-ever-selling new flavour of ice cream when it was first launched. And it's not difficult to understand why – crunchy cream-filled biscuits with rich vanilla and chocolate ice cream is definitely hard to resist.

1 quantity Vanilla Ice Cream (see page 8)

CHOCOLATE COOKIE ICE CREAM:
150 g regular Oreo cookies, crushed
1 quantity Chocolate Ice Cream base (see page 8), chilled

TO FINISH:
3–4 regular Oreo cookies, crumbed
12 mini Oreo cookies
chocolate vermicelli, to sprinkle

an ice cream machine (optional)
4 glass sundae dishes

Serves 4

To make the Chocolate Cookie Ice Cream, churn the Chocolate Ice Cream base in an ice cream machine according to the manufacturer's instructions, or freeze using the by-hand method given on page 6. Just before the ice cream is frozen stir through the crushed Oreo cookies. Freeze until needed.

Layer the Chocolate Cookie Ice Cream, Vanilla Ice Cream and cookie crumbs in the sundae dishes. Sprinkle with chocolate vermicelli and decorate with 3 whole mini Oreo cookies or serve them on the side, if preferred. Serve immediately.

Panna cotta sundae

This is a perfect dinner party dessert. Creamy panna cotta and rosé wine sorbet with raspberries and a shimmer of luxurious gold leaf. Your guests will simply love the popping candy that is hidden beneath the raspberries – an unexpected surprise to transport them back to their childhoods.

ROSÉ WINE SORBET:
250 ml sweet rosé wine
150 g fresh raspberries
100 g caster sugar

PANNA COTTA:
150 ml whole milk
350 ml double cream
1 vanilla pod, split lengthways
60 g caster sugar
2 sheets of leaf gelatine

TO FINISH:
200 g fresh raspberries
sugar syrup or a little melted apricot preserve or jam
gold leaf
3 tablespoons popping candy

an ice cream machine (optional)
6 glass ramekins, pots or tumblers

Serves 6

To make the Rosé Wine Sorbet, put the wine, raspberries, caster sugar and 250 ml water in a saucepan and simmer for about 5 minutes, until the sugar has dissolved and the fruit is very soft. Remove from the heat and press through a fine mesh sieve to remove the raspberry seeds. Leave to cool completely and then churn in an ice cream machine according to the manufacturer's instructions, or freeze using the by-hand method given on page 6. Freeze until needed.

To make the Panna Cotta, simmer the milk and cream in a heavy-based saucepan with the vanilla pod and caster sugar. Leave to infuse for 10 minutes and then remove the vanilla pod. Soak the gelatine in cold water while the cream is infusing, then squeeze out all the water from the gelatine and stir into the warm cream mixture whisking with a small whisk so that the gelatine dissolves. Pour the cream mixture into the glasses through a fine mesh sieve to strain out any undissolved gelatine. Leave to set in the refrigerator for 4–6 hours.

To assemble, brush 6 of the raspberries with a little sugar syrup or melted apricot jam and attach some gold leaf using tweezers or a fine paint brush. Sprinkle ½ tablespoon of popping candy over each panna cotta. Arrange the remaining raspberries on top of the panna cotta, top with a scoop of Rosé Wine Sorbet and garnish each one with a decorated raspberry. Serve immediately.

Rose petal sundae

This sundae, with its perfumed rose ice cream and strawberry-flavoured sorbet will transport you to an English rose garden on a summer's day. Rose syrup comes in a variety of shades of pink – the darker the syrup, the more beautiful the sundae will look. If you can only find a light syrup, try adding a few drops of pink food colouring to obtain a perfect blush-pink colour.

ROSE ICE CREAM:
1 quantity Vanilla Ice Cream base with the vanilla omitted (see page 8)
100 ml rose syrup

SPARKLING STRAWBERRY SORBET:
500 ml sparkling rosé wine
100 ml rose syrup
100 g caster sugar
200 g fresh strawberries, hulled and sliced

TO FINISH:
200 ml double cream, whipped
2 tablespoons rose petal jam
shredded rose petals (pesticide free), to decorate
chopped pistachios, to sprinkle

an ice cream machine (optional)
4 glass sundae dishes

Serves 4

To make the Rose Ice Cream, follow the Vanilla Ice Cream base recipe but replace the vanilla pod with rose syrup. Leave to cool completely and then churn in an ice cream machine according to the manufacturer's instructions, or freeze using the by-hand method given on page 6. Freeze until needed.

To make the Sparkling Strawberry Sorbet, simmer the rosé wine with 100 ml water and the rose syrup, caster sugar and strawberries for 10–15 minutes until the fruit is soft. Strain through a fine mesh sieve, pressing the strawberries down with the back of a spoon to release their juices. Discard the strawberries and allow the wine syrup to cool completely, then churn in an ice cream machine according to the manufacturer's instructions, or freeze using the by-hand method given on page 6. Freeze until needed.

To assemble, gently fold the rose petal jam through the whipped cream. Layer the Rose Ice Cream and Sparkling Strawberry Sorbet in the sundae dishes. Top each one with a scoop of rose-flavoured cream and decorate with a sprinkling of shredded fresh rose petals and chopped pistachios. Serve immediately.

Rocky road sundae

This cheerful combination of nuts, chocolate, marshmallows and glacé cherries is the perfect pick-me-up for anyone with the blues. Said to have been designed originally to cheer people up in the American depression of the 1920s, this sundae is guaranteed to bring a smile to your guests' faces.

MARSHMALLOW ICE CREAM:
1 quantity Vanilla Ice Cream base (see page 8), chilled
55 g mini marshmallows
100 g glacé cherries, chopped
30 g toasted coconut flakes

CHOCOLATE CRUNCH ICE CREAM:
1 quantity Chocolate Ice Cream base (see page 8), chilled
100 g chocolate biscuits, crushed
55 g salted peanuts

TO FINISH:
1 quantity Chocolate Sauce (see page 9)
chocolate vermicelli, to sprinkle
halved glacé cherries, to decorate

an ice cream machine (optional)
4 glass sundae dishes

Serves 4

To make the Marshmallow Ice Cream, churn the Vanilla Ice Cream base in an ice cream machine according to the manufacturer's instructions, or freeze using the by-hand method given on page 6. When almost frozen, stir in the marshmallows, cherries and coconut flakes. Freeze until needed.

To make the Chocolate Crunch Ice Cream, churn the Chocolate Ice Cream base in an ice cream machine according to the manufacturer's instructions, or freeze using the by-hand method given on page 6. When almost frozen, stir in the crushed chocolate biscuits and peanuts. Freeze until needed.

To assemble, put scoops of the Marshmallow Ice Cream in the sundae dishes. Drizzle over some Chocolate Sauce (warmed if liked) and add a scoop of Chocolate Crunch Ice Cream followed by a second scoop of Marshmallow Ice Cream. Sprinkle with chocolate vermicelli and decorate with a few glacé cherries. Serve immediately.

Sticky toffee pudding sundae

Sticky toffee pudding – a much loved family dessert – is simply irresistible served with lashings of hot custard. In the summer, when the weather is too warm for stodgy comfort puddings, why not try this ice cream version instead – creamy toffee ice cream and caramel sorbet, served with chilled fresh custard. The perfect solution.

CARAMEL SORBET:
250 g caster sugar
freshly squeezed juice of 2 lemons
1 teaspoon salt

TOFFEE SWIRL ICE CREAM:
1 quantity Toffee Sauce (see page 9)
1 quantity Vanilla Ice Cream base
(see page 8), chilled

TO FINISH:
300 g ready-made custard, chilled
8 wafer rolls

an ice cream machine (optional)
4 glass sundae dishes

Serves 4

To make the Caramel Sorbet, put the caster sugar in a heavy-based saucepan and melt over gentle heat. Do not stir while the sugar is melting. You need to watch the sugar very carefully – it will take about 5 minutes to melt but once it has melted it can very quickly burn so remove it from the heat as soon as the caramel is a light golden colour. Gently pour in 500 ml water, taking care as the hot caramel may spit. Add the lemon juice and salt. Simmer over low heat for a further 5 minutes and then set aside to cool. Some of the caramel may have formed lumps in the pan but these will dissolve in the water whilst the liquid cools. When cool, churn in an ice cream machine according to the manufacturer's instructions, or freeze using the by-hand method given on page 6. Freeze until needed.

To make the Toffee Swirl Ice Cream, stir 2 tablespoons of the Toffee Sauce into the Vanilla Ice Cream base and churn in an ice cream machine according to the manufacturer's instructions, or freeze using the by-hand method given on page 6. When almost frozen, stir in the remaining toffee sauce to make swirls so that the ice cream becomes rippled with the sauce. Freeze until needed.

Layer the Toffee Swirl Ice Cream, Caramel Sorbet and custard in the sundae dishes and drizzle with the remaining toffee sauce. Add 2 wafer rolls to each sundae or serve on the side. Serve immediately.

Peanut butter sundae

Chocolate and peanut butter make the perfect sweet-and-salty flavour combination. Here peanut butter ice cream is topped with a shard of crunchy peanut brittle and a scoop or two of frozen chocolate yoghurt, which cuts through the sweetness to create the perfect sundae for nut-lovers.

PEANUT BUTTER ICE CREAM:
3 tablespoons crunchy peanut butter
1 quantity Vanilla Ice Cream base
(see page 8), chilled

CHOCOLATE FROZEN YOGHURT:
2 tablespoons cocoa powder, sifted
2 tablespoons light corn syrup
4 tablespoons crunchy peanut butter
500 g Greek yoghurt

PEANUT BRITTLE:
85 g salted peanuts
150 g caster sugar

TO FINISH:
1 quantity Chocolate Sauce (see page 9)
250 ml double cream, whipped
cocoa powder, to dust

an ice cream machine (optional)
a baking tray, lightly greased
4 glass sundae dishes

Serves 4

To make the Peanut Butter Ice Cream, stir the peanut butter into the Vanilla Ice Cream base. Churn in an ice cream machine according to the manufacturer's instructions, or freeze using the by-hand method given on page 6. Freeze until needed.

To make the Chocolate Frozen Yoghurt, stir the cocoa powder, corn syrup and peanut butter into the yoghurt and mix well. Churn in an ice cream machine according to manufacturer's instructions, or freeze using the by-hand method given on page 6. Freeze until needed.

To make the Peanut Brittle, sprinkle the peanuts over the prepared baking tray so that they are close together. Put the caster sugar in a heavy-based saucepan and melt over gentle heat. Melt the sugar gently until just golden brown, taking care not to let it burn. Pour the molten sugar over the peanuts, leave to cool and set and then break into shards.

To assemble, layer the Chocolate Frozen Yoghurt and Peanut Butter Ice Cream in the sundae dishes and drizzle with the chocolate sauce. Top each sundae with a dollop of whipped cream, dust with cocoa powder and decorate with shards of peanut brittle. Serve immediately.

Chocolate brownie sundae

Rich home-made brownies, chocolate ice cream, coffee ice cream studded with chocolate-covered peanuts and lashings of chocolate sauce, make this the ultimate sundae for chocaholics everywhere. It also makes an extra special treat for any birthday celebration when decorated with sparklers.

1 quantity Chocolate Ice Cream
(see page 8)
1 quantity Chocolate Sauce (see page 9)

COFFEE ICE CREAM:

2 tablespoons instant coffee granules
1 tablespoon boiling water
1 quantity Vanilla Ice Cream base
(see page 8), chilled
135 g white- and milk-chocolate
covered peanuts, plus extra to decorate

CHOCOLATE BROWNIES:

125 g unsalted butter, melted
and cooled
200 g dark chocolate, melted and cooled
3 eggs
250 g caster sugar
125 g plain flour, sifted
100 g macadamia nuts, chopped
100 g milk chocolate chips

an *ice cream machine (optional)*
a *20 x 25 cm brownie tin, greased*
4 glass sundae dishes

Serves 4

To make the Coffee Ice Cream, dissolve the instant coffee granules in the boiling water and leave to cool. Stir the dissolved coffee through the Vanilla Ice Cream base and freeze in an ice cream machine according to the manufacturer's instructions, or freeze using the by-hand method given on page 6. When the ice cream is almost frozen, stir in the chocolate-covered peanuts. Freeze until needed.

To make the Chocolate Brownies, preheat the oven to 190°C (375°F) Gas 5. Put the melted butter and chocolate in a bowl and mix. In a separate large bowl, whisk together the eggs and caster sugar until light, creamy and doubled in volume. Add the flour, melted chocolate and butter mixture, macadamia nuts and chocolate chips to the egg and sugar mixture and fold in with a spatula until the mixture is evenly mixed. Scrape the brownie mixture into the prepared baking tin using a spatula. Bake in the preheated oven for 35–40 minutes, until the brownie has a crust on top but is still soft in the centre. Allow to cool in the tin before transferring to a wire rack to cool completely and cutting into small squares.

Place a square or two of brownie at the base of each sundae dish and top with scoops of Chocolate Ice Cream and Coffee Ice Cream. Drizzle with Chocolate Sauce and sprinkle with some chocolate-covered peanuts. Serve immediately.

Note: You can store any leftover brownies in an airtight container for up to 5 days.

RETRO

Summer berry parfait

This classic sundae is a delectable combination of vanilla ice cream with summer berries and fluffy whipped cream. I've added a tangy strawberry vanilla sorbet here to give it an extra summery feel, but you could replace it with the Strawberry Ice Cream on page 8 for an even more indulgent treat.

1 quantity Vanilla Ice Cream (see page 8)
350 g fresh strawberries, hulled and sliced if large
400 g fresh raspberries
1 quantity Summer Berry Sauce (see page 9)

STRAWBERRY VANILLA SORBET:
450 g fresh strawberries, hulled
200 g caster sugar
freshly squeezed juice of 1 lemon
1 vanilla pod, split lengthways

TO FINISH:
300 ml double cream, whipped
4 fresh strawberries, hulls attached, to decorate

an ice cream machine (optional)
4 glass sundae dishes

Serves 4

To make the Strawberry Vanilla Sorbet, chop the strawberries and put them in a saucepan with 500 ml water, the caster sugar, lemon juice and vanilla pod. Simmer over gentle heat for about 10–15 minutes, until the fruit is very soft. Leave to cool completely and then blitz to a smooth purée with a hand-held blender. Churn in an ice cream machine according to the manufacturer's instructions, or freeze using the by-hand method given on page 6. Freeze until needed.

To assemble, layer the strawberries and raspberries in the sundae glasses with scoops of Vanilla Ice Cream, Strawberry Vanilla Sorbet and Summer Berry sauce. Top the sundaes with a swirl of whipped cream, and decorate each one with a fresh strawberry. Serve immediately.

Classic banana split

The grand-daddy of all sundaes — this American classic harks back to the days when bananas were a special treat rather than an everyday fruit. I think it's the outrageous three-sauces, three-flavours of ice cream combination that makes it so irresistibly delicious!

4 large ripe bananas

4 scoops each of Vanilla, Chocolate and Strawberry Ice Cream (see page 8)

4 tablespoons each of Chocolate, Toffee and Summer Berry Sauce (see page 9)

TO FINISH:
250 ml whipping cream, whipped
4 tablespoons chopped mixed nuts
12 glacé cherries, halved
4 fan wafers

an ice cream machine (optional)
4 banana split boat dishes

Serves 4

Peel the bananas and cut them in half lengthways. Arrange split-side up in the dishes. Put 3 scoops of ice cream, in different flavours, down the length of the each banana, between the 2 halves. Drizzle the 3 sauces generously over the top.

Spoon the whipped cream over the ice cream. Sprinkle liberally with chopped nuts and top with glacé cherries. Set the wafers in the ice cream at a jaunty angle, like the sails of a boat. Serve immediately.

Hot rum and raisin split

In a variation on the classic, why not try a split made with warm baked bananas? Preheat the oven to 190°C (375°F) Gas 5. Peel 4 bananas and place them in the centre of a large double layer of foil. Carefully pour over half a quantity of Toffee Sauce (see page 9) and 3 tablespoons dark rum and sprinkle over 3 tablespoons raisins. Fold the foil over the bananas and seal tightly. Place the parcel on a baking tray and bake in the preheated oven for 15–18 minutes. Let cool slightly, unwrap and then cut in half lengthways and place in banana split boat dishes. Top with scoops of Vanilla Ice Cream (see page 8), swirls of whipped cream and the remaining toffee sauce. Serve immediately.

Banoffee split

If you love bananas, this sundae is simply irresistible! In a new twist on the more familiar Banana Split (see page 41), this version combines the traditional elements but uses rich banana and cinnamon ice creams, toffee and chocolate sauces and is topped with dried banana chips and walnuts. Yum.

4 ripe bananas

1 quantity Cinnamon Ice Cream (see page 18)

4 tablespoons each of Toffee Sauce and Chocolate Sauce (see page 9)

BANANA ICE CREAM:

2 ripe bananas

freshly squeezed juice of 1 lemon

1 quantity Vanilla Ice Cream base (see page 8), chilled

TO FINISH:

dried banana chips, to sprinkle

chopped walnut halves, to sprinkle

an ice cream machine (optional)

4 banana split boat dishes

Serves 4

To make the Banana Ice Cream, put the bananas in a bowl with the lemon juice and use a fork to mash them to a smooth paste. Fold the banana mixture into the Vanilla Ice Cream base and churn in an ice cream machine according to the manufacturer's instructions, or freeze using the by-hand method given on page 6. Freeze until needed.

To assemble, peel the bananas and cut them in half lengthways. Arrange split-side up in the dishes. Put 1 scoop of Cinnamon Ice Cream and 2 scoops Banana Ice Cream, down the length of the each banana, between the 2 halves.

Drizzle the Toffee Sauce and Chocolate Sauce generously over the top. Sprinkle with banana chips and walnuts to finish. Serve immediately.

Strawberry shortcake sundae

Buttery home-made shortcake, juicy fresh strawberries and a rich strawberry and clotted cream ice cream make up this heavenly sundae. If you don't have time to make the shortcake yourself, use a shop-bought biscuit instead – Scottish petticoat tail shortbreads work well.

STRAWBERRY AND CLOTTED CREAM ICE CREAM:

160 g caster sugar

2 eggs

225 g clotted cream

250 ml double cream

250 ml whole milk

400 g fresh strawberries, hulled and chopped

SHORTCAKE:

60 g caster sugar

120 g unsalted butter

185 g plain flour, sifted

TO FINISH:

400 g fresh strawberries, hulled and sliced

250 ml double cream, whipped

1 quantity Summer Berry Sauce (see page 9)

an ice cream machine (optional)
2 large baking trays, greased and lined with baking paper
an 8-cm round biscuit cutter

Serves 4

To make the Strawberry and Clotted Cream Ice Cream, put the caster sugar, eggs, clotted cream, double cream, milk and strawberries in a blender and blitz for a few minutes until you have a smooth mixture. Churn in an ice cream machine according to the manufacturer's instructions, or freeze using the by-hand method given on page 6. Freeze until needed.

To make the Shortcake, preheat the oven to 180°C (350°F) Gas 4. Cream together the caster sugar and butter and then mix in the flour to form a soft dough, adding a little milk if the mixture is too dry. Wrap the dough in clingfilm and chill in the refrigerator for 1 hour. Roll out the dough on a floured work surface to a thickness of about 5 mm. Use the biscuit cutter to stamp out 16 rounds. Carefully transfer the rounds to the prepared baking trays and bake in the preheated oven for 10–12 minutes until golden brown. Leave to cool completely.

To assemble, put a generous layer of sliced strawberries and Summer Berry Sauce in the sundae dishes. Add a scoop of Strawberry and Clotted Cream Ice Cream, follow with a large dollop of whipped cream and finish with another scoop of the ice cream. Drizzle with the remaining sauce and decorate with a Shortcake or serve the biscuits on the side if preferred.

Note: You can store any leftover Shortcake in an airtight container for up to 5 days.

Trifle sundae

Everyone loves a traditional trifle – fruity jelly, sherry-soaked sponge cake and creamy egg custard. The addition here of a layer of rich vanilla ice cream takes this favourite family dessert to a new level. For a child-friendly version, replace the sherry with unsweetened apple juice.

100 g raspberry jelly cubes
6 ready-made trifle sponges
150 ml sherry
200 g fresh raspberries
1 quantity Vanilla Ice Cream
(see page 8)
400 g ready-made custard, chilled
250 ml whipping cream, whipped
hundreds and thousands, to sprinkle

an ice cream machine (optional)
4 glass sundae dishes
a piping bag fitted with a large
star nozzle

Serves 6

Make the raspberry jelly following the packet instructions and leave to cool slightly.

Place a trifle sponge into the bottom of each dish, pressing down so they fit snugly. Pour the sherry over the trifle sponges and top each sponge with a quarter of the raspberries. Pour over the cooled raspberry jelly and carefully transfer to the refrigerator to set.

To assemble, bring the Vanilla Ice Cream to room temperature so that it is fairly soft. Place a spoonful of ice cream on top of each jelly and level the surface with the back of a spoon to create an even layer. Cover the ice cream with a layer of chilled custard.

Put the whipped cream in the prepared piping bag and pipe little stars of cream all over the top of each trifle. Sprinkle with hundreds and thousands to decorate. Serve immediately.

Lemon meringue pie sundae

Lemon meringue pie is one of my favourite desserts – my mother used to make it for dinner parties when we were little and, as a special treat, we would be allowed any leftovers for breakfast the next morning! The meringue topping shown here was finished off with a cook's blow torch but if you don't have one, buy meringues nests, crush them and sprinkle them over the top of the sundaes.

LEMON CURD ICE CREAM:
2 eggs
225 g clotted cream
250 ml double cream
250 ml whole milk
160 g caster sugar
300 g lemon curd

GIN AND LEMON SORBET:
5 unwaxed lemons
100 ml dry gin
200 g caster sugar

MERINGUE TOPPING:
2 egg whites
4 tablespoons caster sugar

TO FINISH:
150 g digestive biscuits, crumbed
60 g unsalted butter, melted
3 tablespoons white mini marshmallows
100 g lemon curd

an ice cream machine (optional)
4 glass sundae dishes
a cook's blow torch (optional)

Serves 4

To make the Lemon Curd Ice Cream, put the eggs, clotted cream, double cream, milk, caster sugar and lemon curd in a blender and blitz until smooth. Churn in an ice cream machine according to the manufacturer's instructions, or freeze using the by-hand method given on page 6. Freeze until needed.

To make the Gin and Lemon Sorbet, finely grate the zest from 2 of the lemons and place in a saucepan with the juice of all 5 lemons. Add the gin, 500 ml water and the caster sugar. Simmer over gentle heat for 5–10 minutes until the sugar has dissolved and you have a thin lemon syrup. Leave to cool completely, chill and then churn in an ice cream machine according to the manufacturer's instructions, or freeze using the by-hand method on page 6. Freeze until needed.

To assemble, mix together the biscuit crumbs and melted butter and divide between the sundae glasses. Sprinkle in a few mini marshmallows and top with a scoop each of the Gin and Lemon Sorbet and Lemon Curd Ice Cream and spoon in some lemon curd. Return the sundaes to the freezer while you make the meringue topping (but only briefly).

To make the meringue topping, put the egg whites in a grease-free bowl and whisk until stiff. Gradually whisk in the caster sugar 1 tablespoonful at a time until the mixture is very stiff and glossy. Spoon a quarter of the meringue on top of each sundae and carefully brown with a cook's blow torch until the peaks are brown. (Alternatively, sprinkle the top of each sundae with crushed meringue nest.) Serve immediately.

Neapolitan Sundae

This combination of strawberry, vanilla and chocolate ice creams is a timeless classic. Although ready-made blocks of striped Neapolitan ice cream are available to buy, these can't compete with the divine result you get by using your own creamy home-made ice creams and sticky sauces.

1 quantity each of Vanilla, Strawberry and Chocolate Ice Cream (see page 8)

125 ml each of Summer Berry, Toffee and Chocolate Sauce (see page 9)

DECORATED WAFERS:

55 g white chocolate

4 large fan wafers

hundreds and thousands

an ice cream machine (optional)
greaseproof paper
4 glass sundae dishes

Serves 4

To make the decorated wafers, break the white chocolate into pieces and place in a heatproof bowl set over a saucepan of barely simmering water. Heat until the chocolate has melted – it's important that the bottom of the bowl does not touch the water – if it does the chocolate will overheat and spoil. Allow the chocolate to cool slightly and then spoon onto a plate. Roll the top edge of each wafer in the chocolate so that it is thickly coated and then sprinkle with hundreds and thousands. Place the wafers on greaseproof paper and leave the chocolate to set.

To assemble, spoon a little Summer Berry Sauce into the sundae dishes. Add a scoop of Vanilla Ice Cream followed by a layer of Toffee Sauce. Next add a scoop of Strawberry Ice Cream followed by a layer of Chocolate Sauce and top with a scoop of Chocolate Ice Cream. Insert a wafer into the top of each sundae to finish. Serve immediately.

Mint choc chip sundae

Mint choc chip ice cream was hugely popular in the 1970s when ice cream flavours were limited and it's easy to understand why as it's the perfect taste combination. This sundae makes a great end to a dinner party as it allows you to serve your guests 'after dinner' mints as part of the dessert.

MINT SORBET:
300 g caster sugar
freshly squeezed juice of 1 lemon
20 g fresh mint, finely chopped
1 teaspoon green food colouring

MINT CHOC CHIP ICE CREAM:
1 quantity Vanilla Ice Cream base (see page 8), chilled
1 teaspoon mint essence
100 g mint chocolate sticks, finely chopped
1 teaspoon green food colouring

MINT CHOC SAUCE:
150 g peppermint fondant-filled chocolate squares (such as After Eights)
250 ml double cream

TO FINISH:
4 mint chocolate sticks

an ice cream machine (optional)
4 glass sundae dishes

Serves 4

To make the Mint Sorbet, put the caster sugar, lemon juice, fresh mint and green food colouring in a saucepan with 600 ml water. Simmer for 10 minutes until the sugar has dissolved and you have a thin mint syrup. Strain through a fine mesh sieve to remove the mint and leave to cool. When completely cool, churn in an ice cream machine according to the manufacturer's instructions, or freeze using the by-hand method given on page 6. Freeze until needed.

To make the Mint Choc Chip Ice Cream, add the mint essence, chopped mint chocolate sticks and 1 teaspoon green food colouring to the Vanilla Ice Cream base and churn in an ice cream machine according to the manufacturer's instructions, or freeze using the by-hand method given on page 6. Freeze until needed.

To make the Mint Choc Sauce, place the peppermint squares and double cream in a saucepan and set over gentle heat. Stir until the mints have melted and the sauce is thick and glossy. Leave to cool completely.

To assemble, layer the Chocolate Mint Sauce, Mint Choc Chip Ice Cream and Mint Sorbet in the sundae dishes. Decorate each sundae with a mint chocolate stick. Serve immediately.

GROWN-UP

Rum and raisin sundae

Plump raisins laced with rum, silky smooth rum and raisin ice cream and rich chocolate brownies all come together deliciously to create this indulgent sundae. This is definitely one for adults only!

4 large shop-bought or home-made chocolate brownies (see page 37)
250 ml double cream, whipped

RUM AND RAISIN ICE CREAM:
200 g raisins, soaked overnight in 250 ml dark rum
1 quantity Vanilla Ice Cream base (see page 8), chilled
150 g shop-bought rum and raisin fudge, finely chopped

an ice cream machine (optional)
4 glass sundae dishes
a piping bag fitted with a very large star nozzle

Serves 4

For the Rum and Raisin Ice Cream, stir half the rum-soaked raisins into the Vanilla Ice Cream base together with most of the chopped fudge (reserving a little for decoration) and churn in an ice cream machine according to manufacturer's instructions, or freeze using the by-hand method given on page 6. Freeze until needed.

To assemble, place half a brownie in the bottom of each sundae dish. Spoon over some of the reserved rum-soaked raisins and rum and top with a scoop of Rum and Raisin Ice Cream and a spoonful of whipped cream. Place the remaining brownies halves on top, follow with a further scoop of ice cream and pipe a large swirl of whipped cream on top. Sprinkle over a few rum-soaked raisins and the remaining chopped fudge. Serve immediately.

Vin Santo sundae

The rich flavours of Vin Santo wine always transport me to the hills of Tuscany. Served here with ripe nectarines and creamy honeycomb ice cream, this is a summer's day delight and would make the perfect ending to an *al fresco* lunch. Serve the remaining Vin Santo from the bottle to accompany the sundaes if you wish.

4 ripe nectarines, halved and stoned
crushed honeycomb, to sprinkle

NECTARINE SORBET:
4 ripe nectarines, halved, stoned and roughly chopped
200 ml Vin Santo
freshly squeezed juice of 1 lemon
100 g caster sugar

HONEYCOMB ICE CREAM:
150 g honeycomb, broken into pieces
1 quantity Vanilla Ice Cream base (see page 8), chilled

an ice cream machine (optional)
4 glass sundae dishes

Serves 4

First poach all 8 of the nectarines for the sundae and for the Nectarine Sorbet. Put the nectarine halves and the chopped nectarine flesh in a large saucepan together with the Vin Santo, lemon juice, caster sugar and 500 ml water. Simmer over gentle heat for 15–20 minutes until the fruit is soft. Set the pan aside to cool completely. When cool, remove the nectarine halves with a slotted spoon and store in the refrigerator with a little of the poaching liquid until you are ready to serve the sundaes.

To make the Nectarine Sorbet, purée the remaining poached nectarine flesh and poaching liquid in a blender to a smooth pulp. Churn in an ice cream machine according to manufacturer's instructions, or freeze using the by-hand method given on page 6. Freeze until needed.

To make the Honeycomb Ice Cream, fold the pieces of honeycomb into the Vanilla Ice Cream base and churn in an ice cream machine according to the manufacturer's instructions, or freeze using the by-hand method given on page 6. Freeze until needed.

To assemble, place 2 poached nectarine halves in the bottom of each sundae dish and top with scoops of Honeycomb Ice Cream and Nectarine Sorbet. Sprinkle with crushed honeycomb to decorate and serve immediately with a small glass of Vin Santo on the side, if liked.

Egg Nog sundae

On cold wintry days, there is nothing nicer than warming up by a crackling fire sipping a cup of nutmeg-scented egg nog. This indulgent sundae is packed full of festive flavours, including cinnamon, spiced gingerbread, candied pecans and ice cream flavoured with Advocaat liqueur, which has a hint of warming brandy. Who says an ice cream sundae is just for summer?

CANDIED PECANS:

1 egg white

100 g caster sugar

1 teaspoon ground cinnamon

50 g unsalted butter, melted

1 teaspoon vanilla extract

150 g pecan pieces

EGG NOG ICE CREAM:

1 quantity Vanilla Ice Cream base with the vanilla omitted (see page 8), chilled

160 ml Advocaat liqueur

candied pecans (see above)

TO FINISH:

4 thick slices ready-made Jamaican Ginger Cake or moist gingerbread

300 ml double cream, whipped

freshly grated or ground nutmeg, to dust

an ice cream machine (optional)
a baking tray, lightly greased
4 glass sundae dishes
a 5-cm round biscuit cutter

Serves 4

To make the Candied Pecans, preheat the oven to 150°C (300°F) Gas 2. Whisk the egg white to stiff peaks. Slowly whisk in the caster sugar 1 tablespoonful at a time, then add the cinnamon, melted butter and vanilla extract. Fold the pecans into the meringue mixture and turn the mixture out onto the prepared baking tray. Bake in the preheated oven for 25–30 minutes, stirring the nuts every 10 minutes or so initially and then more frequently towards the end of cooking, until the coating on the nuts is crisp. Set aside to cool.

To make the Egg Nog Ice Cream, stir the Advocaat liqueur into the Vanilla Ice Cream base. Churn in an ice cream machine according to the manufacturer's instruction, or freeze using the by-hand method given on page 6. When almost frozen, stir in two-thirds of the candied pecans. Freeze until needed.

To assemble, place a scoop of Egg Nog Ice Cream in the bottom of the sundae dishes. Use the biscuit cutter to stamp out 4 small rounds from the ginger cake and place one in each sundae dish. Top with a second scoop of the ice cream and sprinkle over some of the remaining candied pecans. Cover with a swirl of whipped cream and decorate with a few more candied pecans and a pinch of nutmeg. Serve immediately.

Tiramisù sundae

'Tiramisù' translated from the Italian means 'pick-me-up' and perfectly describes the elements of this dessert – rich strong coffee with a caffeine hit, creamy mascarpone ice cream and the essential dusting of cocoa powder. To make the dessert look like a classic tiramisù, the ice cream needs to be softened slightly when you assemble the sundae. This is best done straight from churning in the ice cream machine or if using the by-hand method, remove from the freezer to soften before use.

3 tablespoons instant coffee granules
250 ml boiling water
150 ml coffee liqueur (such as Tia Maria)
8 sponge fingers (savoiardi biscuits)
55 g dark chocolate chips
cocoa powder, for dusting

MASCARPONE ICE CREAM:
250 g mascarpone cheese
200 ml crème fraîche
200 ml double cream
2 tablespoons icing sugar, sifted

an ice cream machine (optional)
4 glass sundae dishes or wine glasses

Serves 4

Dissolve the coffee granules in the boiling water. Add the coffee liqueur and leave to cool completely.

To make the Mascarpone Ice Cream, mix together the mascarpone cheese, crème fraîche and double cream and stir in the icing sugar. Churn in an ice cream machine according to the manufacturer's instructions, or freeze using the by-hand method given on page 6.

To assemble, break 4 of the sponge fingers into pieces and arrange them in the bottom of each of the sundae dishes. Drizzle with a little of the coffee liquid until moist. Sprinkle a few chocolate chips over each one and dust with cocoa. Place a spoonful of the softened Mascarpone Ice Cream into each dish and level the surface with the back of a spoon. Arrange the remaining sponge fingers on top and drizzle over a little more of the coffee liquid. Sprinkle with a few more chocolate chips, add a further dusting of cocoa powder and top with the remaining Mascarpone Ice Cream, again levelling the surface with a spoon or pallette knife. Dust the top of each sundae liberally with cocoa powder and serve immediately.

Black forest sundae

The classic gateaux from the Schwarzwald in Germany is the inspiration for this sophisticated sundae. It's a modern update on the favourite 1970s dinner party dessert – moist chocolate sponge, cherries, cream and of course the obligatory kirsch liqueur make this sundae a cherry lover's delight.

1 quantity Chocolate Ice Cream
(see page 8)

2 ready-made chocolate muffins,
cut into cubes

4 tablespoons kirsch

200 g stoned morello cherries in syrup

300 ml double cream, whipped

55 g dark chocolate, coarsely grated

4 fresh cherries, to decorate

CHERRY RIPPLE ICE CREAM:

1 quantity Vanilla Ice Cream base
(see page 8), chilled

4 tablespoons cherry jam or preserve

an ice cream machine (optional)
4 glass sundae dishes
a piping bag fitted with a very large
star nozzle

Serves 4

To make the Cherry Ripple Ice Cream, churn the Vanilla Ice Cream base in an ice cream machine according to the manufacturer's instructions, or freeze using the by-hand method given on page 6. When the ice cream is almost frozen, add the cherry jam and stir through gently in swirls so that the ice cream becomes rippled with the jam. Freeze until needed.

To assemble, arrange some cubes of chocolate muffin in the bottom of each sundae dish. Spoon 1 tablespoon of kirsch over each one and divide the morello cherries between the sundae dishes. Top with scoops of Cherry Ripple Ice Cream and Chocolate Ice Cream.

Put the whipped cream in the piping bag and pipe a large swirl on top of each sundae. Sprinkle with grated chocolate and a top with a fresh cherry to decorate. Serve immediately.

Index